DUFFY
BOOKS IN HOMES
USA

This "Duffy" Book
was generously provided by
Corporate Partners:

CaroTrans
and
MAINFREIGHT USA

www.DuffyBooksInHomesUSA.org

D1214472

AMENDMENTS TO THE UNITED STATES CONSTITUTION
THE BILL OF RIGHTS

THE RIGHT TO A JURY TRIAL

KATHY FURGANG

rosen publishing's
rosen
central®

New York

Published in 2011 by The Rosen Publishing Group, Inc.
29 East 21st Street, New York, NY 10010

Copyright © 2011 by The Rosen Publishing Group, Inc.

First Edition

Library of Congress Cataloging-in-Publication Data

Furgang, Kathy.
The Seventh Amendment: the right to a jury trial/Kathy Furgang.
    p. cm. — (Amendments to the United States Constitution: the Bill of Rights)
Includes bibliographical references and index.
ISBN 978-1-4488-1262-2 (library binding)
ISBN 978-1-4488-2308-6 (pbk.)
ISBN 978-1-4488-2318-5 (6-pack)
1. United States. Constitution. 7th Amendment—Juvenile literature. 2. Jury—United States—Juvenile literature. I. Title.
KF8972.F87 2011
347.73'52—dc22

2010017696

Manufactured in the United States of America

CPSIA Compliance Information: Batch #W11YA: For further information, contact Rosen Publishing, New York, New York, at 1-800-237-9932.

On the cover: A lawyer questions a witness and gathers testimony during a civil case before a jury. Bottom right: A defendant receives advice from his lawyer as a jury looks on. The right to a jury trial in civil cases is guaranteed by the Seventh Amendment.

CONTENTS

INTRODUCTION

I n Boston, Massachusetts, a woman named Alyssa Burrage spent close to a half million dollars buying a condominium. Yet she soon found that the secondhand smoke from her downstairs neighbor aggravated her asthma. So instead of enjoying her new condo, Burrage became ill and had trouble breathing in her own home.

The smoke had not come as a complete surprise to Burrage. While visiting the condo before purchasing it, she had noticed the smell of cigarette smoke. Her real estate broker, representing Gibson Sotheby's International Realty, told her that the person who was selling the place must be a smoker and that the smell would go away once the person

A jury's job is to help decide what is fair and settle disputes between parties. Attorneys for the plaintiffs and defendants argue the case before the jury members.

moved out. But that was not what happened. When Burrage found out that the smoke was coming from her neighbor's condo below, she felt that her broker had misled her.

What rights does a homeowner have in a situation like this? Is the broker to blame for Burrage's problem? What compensation, if any, does she deserve? In the United States, there is a branch of the legal system that deals with such disputes between individuals, as well as disputes between individuals and organizations. This branch of law is called civil law. When there is money involved in these civil law disputes, the citizens are guaranteed a formal hearing to decide what should be done.

The ten original amendments to the U.S. Constitution, all of them proposed in 1789 and ratified in 1791, are known collectively as the Bill of Rights. One of these is the Seventh Amendment. Thanks to the Seventh Amendment, a trial by jury is guaranteed in civil disputes involving more than $20. A jury is a group of citizens assigned to make an honest and objective decision after hearing all of the information in a case. Juries are one of the most important aspects of our legal system. As Americans, we respect the decisions of juries and abide by them.

Alyssa Burrage sued her real estate broker to help to settle her dispute. The jury listened to both parties in the case for an entire week. When the jurors finally made their decision, however, they sided with the real estate broker, so Burrage did not win her case.

Although Burrage did not receive money as compensation for her complaint, the case did bring the problem of secondhand smoke to the general public's attention. This is likely to make real estate brokers more careful in the future about what they say or don't say to potential buyers. It will probably also make potential buyers ask more questions and inspect properties more carefully before purchasing them. So even though Burrage did not win her case, something good still came out of it.

As Americans, we are constantly learning important lessons from the issues investigated and debated in civil cases. And the precedents set in these cases influence how similar cases are decided in the future. Since the late 1700s, the Seventh Amendment has helped ordinary citizens work with the American legal system to settle disputes that ultimately affect all of our lives.

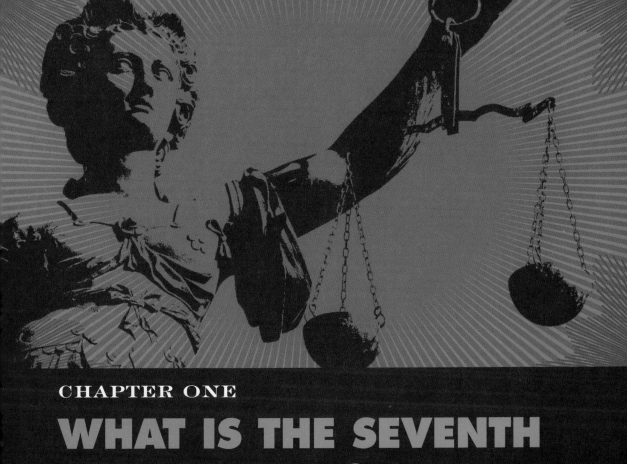

CHAPTER ONE

WHAT IS THE SEVENTH AMENDMENT?

Today, if we have a problem with another person, a company, or the law, we know that we can bring our complaint or tell our side of the story to a judge and jury and feel reasonably certain that justice will be served. We trust that this system works, and we are willing to accept the consequences if the outcome is not in our favor.

In law, a plaintiff is a person who brings a case or complaint against someone else in a court of law. The defendant is the person who is being accused of wrongdoing or having done something unfair. Civil cases are ones that do not involve crimes. The outcome of the trial will not result in imprisonment. Rather, the jury is deciding if the defendant is responsible for the misdeeds he or she is accused of and therefore liable to

QUIET PLEASE

COURT MEDIATION	JUDGE CATHERINE M. POOLER	612 →
COURT MEDIATION	JUDGE SHELLEY J. KRAVITZ	615 →
OOM		

The parties involved in a dispute must abide by the decision of a jury. This couple sits in a Miami, Florida, courthouse, waiting for a jury to arrive at a decision concerning custody of their four-year-old daughter.

penalty. The penalty is usually financial, and money is paid to the plaintiff as compensation. Civil cases often involve disputes over property or cases in which people think they have been treated unfairly for some reason.

Civil cases include divorce, alimony, child custody and child support, personal injuries, wrongful death, libel or slander, medical malpractice, contract disputes, or property disputes. A civil dispute might be between neighbors or between an employee and employer. It might even be between friends or family members. Sometimes, civil cases can be based upon a dispute between an individual and a corporation. The case is considered civil because the plaintiff is not accusing the defendant of a crime, but merely trying to settle a dispute. The plaintiff is often seeking an admission of wrongdoing and/or compensation, rather than criminal punishment.

The right to a fair trial with a jury is taken for granted today. This was not always the case in America. Back in the days when England ruled the American colonies, laws and the legal system were much different. The American colonists were forced to follow British laws, but these were often not enforced properly and the rights of the colonists were not considered. The idea of a fair trial by a jury of one's peers did not exist in colonial America. In fact, many of the trials back then were downright unfair.

The Salem Witch Trials

Between February 1692 and May 1693, in the town of Salem, Massachusetts, innocent people were put to death because of an unfair legal system. During this time, many people in several Massachusetts counties were accused of witchcraft. Not much evidence was needed to accuse or convict someone of this very serious charge, which could bring the death penalty.

The accused were given trials before the local magistrates, who were officers, judges, or officials in the town. The magistrates in power in the

1600s were not the fair and impartial judges that we know today. Many magistrates forced the accused into making false confessions. The accused were also encouraged to make false accusations of witchcraft against other innocent citizens. By the time the Salem witchcraft ordeal was over, more than 150 people had been arrested and placed in prisons. Some were left to die in jail, while others were given trials unlike any we know today.

If anyone accused a person of witchcraft, that person was simply arrested and pressured by the magistrate to confess. Odd tests were developed to determine if someone was a witch. Sometimes the accused were asked to recite a prayer. They were found guilty if they could not recite it flawlessly and without stumbling over the words. Another test involved a cake made from the urine of the accused and then eaten by a dog. It was believed that the accused would feel pain when the dog ate the cake, and this pain would identify the person as a witch.

Not every person on trial in Salem was found guilty of witchcraft. However, more than twenty-five people were put to death, and cruel and unusual measures were taken to force confessions. One eighty-year-old man who would not confess had heavy rocks placed on his chest for

The Salem witch trials of the early 1690s are an infamous example of how unjust judicial systems can inflict pain and suffering—and even death—on innocent people.

several days. The man still refused to confess and eventually died under the continued pressure of the rocks.

The Salem witch trials are an extreme example of a time in our country's history when legal trials were anything but fair. As the years

passed, lawyers began to hear cases in front of professional judges sworn to uphold the legal system and the cause of justice. Yet even these judges could occasionally be corrupted. Rather than remaining objective (evenhanded and neutral) and deciding cases based solely on matters of law and justice, some judges ruled based on their own personal biases or to help friends or business associates. In these cases, it was very difficult to prove that the hearings were unjust. And the ruling of the judge, no matter how corrupt and unfair, was the final word.

Types of Trials Throughout History

Before trial by a jury of one's peers was instituted, making a judicial decision of guilt or innocence was often a difficult and sometimes deadly process. In medieval times, in particular, the judicial process was far different from the American justice system in place today.

Trial by ordeal was a judicial process in which an accused person was deliberately placed in a dangerous situation. The accused person either confessed to the crime (honestly or falsely) in order to end the ordeal, or he or she refused to confess. If no confession was offered, but the accused survived the ordeal, he or she would be proven innocent. In a trial by combat, the two parties in a dispute dueled or battled each other, sometimes to the death. The winner of the battle was declared the winner of the case. In a trial by oath, God-fearing subjects were placed under oath by, for example, swearing to tell the truth while placing one hand on the Bible. They were then asked to swear to their innocence. If the accused person lied under oath, it was believed that he or she would be subject to God's wrath and eternal punishment and damnation. Even today, when witnesses and suspects take the stand to testify, they swear an oath of truthfulness. Anyone convicted of lying under oath is convicted of perjury and subject to jail time.

The Case of Crispus Attucks

In the years leading up to the American Revolution, trial juries had become more common in helping to decide whether a defendant was guilty or not guilty. Just before the outbreak of the American Revolution, the Boston Massacre occurred.

Boston patriots protesting the Townshend Act (which taxed colonists to help pay the salaries of colonial governors and judges) were being watched over by British soldiers. The soldiers were trying to keep peace in the increasingly tense and volatile capital city of the rebellious Massachusetts colony. When the protesters became unruly, soldiers fired their guns into the crowd. The first to die in this incident was a colonist named Crispus Attucks. Several other men died that day as well, and the British soldiers were brought to trial on murder charges.

Even though he was a leading patriot deeply committed to the struggle against British oppression, the attorney and future American president John Adams defended the British soldiers. He took their case in order to prove that everyone deserves a good legal defense and a fair trial. It was this commitment to fairness and justice, Adams argued, that set Americans apart from their British oppressors. Several months passed before the trial was held, so that public outrage and fury could die down a bit. It was also held in another town to ensure that the jurors chosen would be impartial, or completely fair and objective in their judgment.

Adams argued that many of the soldiers acted to protect themselves because they believed their lives were being threatened by the crowd of angry protesters. Yet two of the soldiers were found guilty of murder because they fired directly into the crowd rather than firing warning shots. However, these men did not suffer any punishment more severe than receiving a branding on their thumbs.

An unfair system is what kept these two soldiers from being convicted of murder and sentenced to death. The colonies were subject to British common law. This meant that if there was a precedent, or a previous case that was similar, the decision made in that earlier case could be applied to the

This is a historical depiction of the Boston Massacre, which caused the death of Crispus Attucks and other colonists. The civil case that followed was seen by many colonists as a failure of justice, since the soldiers involved in the shooting did not receive the usual punishment due convicted murderers.

current one. Adams was aware of an odd loophole in British common law. Any first-time offender who could prove he was literate—by reading a chosen passage from the Bible—could receive a lesser punishment for the crime of which he stood accused. Once applicable only to clergy members, this loophole, known as the Benefit of Clergy, was eventually expanded to cover any first-time offender who could read. Adams had the two soldiers who had been convicted of murder read from the Bible before the court. Having successfully done so, they received the lesser sentence of manslaughter and the lesser punishment of branding.

English common-law precedents, like the one used to settle this murder trial, relied on broad and very generic guidelines, rather than on the specifics and evidence of the case being tried. And in nearly all such cases, common-law decisions and precedents favored the British crown over the rights and interests of the colonists.

A Need for Change

After the American Revolution, it was time for the United States of America to establish its own system of rules and laws to help govern the new country. The Articles of Confederation was the original constitution of the United States. It would later be replaced by the U.S. Constitution, ratified in 1788.

Yet almost immediately, it was recognized that even this new and improved Constitution needed some revisions and enhancements that

would provide for better protection of citizens' rights and make the extent and limits of government powers clearer. These changes became a group of ten amendments, called the Bill of Rights. Today there are twenty-seven amendments to the Constitution, but those original ten

remain among the most important to the formation of our country and its ideals.

The Seventh Amendment was designed to make civil trials as fair and impartial as possible, avoiding the kind of corruption and injustice that often characterized the application of British common law in the colonial era. While many of the amendments contained within the Bill of Rights were strongly debated by politicians and ordinary citizens of the time, the Seventh Amendment did not meet with much opposition. It was generally agreed upon that an impartial jury system would help improve the cause of justice and fairness in the new country.

A jury system was widely thought of as a good way to remove considerations of class, wealth, and influence from trials. In theory, the rich, powerful, and educated would not receive any special consideration or leniency, and the poor, powerless, and uneducated would not be victimized by authority. A jury of average citizens taking part in the process and making a decision

It was not until the Seventh Amendment was ratified and went into effect that civil cases were constitutionally guaranteed to be argued, deliberated, and decided in a fair and impartial way, as shown in this 1852 painting of a Missouri courtroom.

based upon careful weighing of evidence would help to maintain fairness for all people brought before a court.

Even Samuel Bryan of Pennsylvania, a member of the Anti-Federalist party that opposed many of the constitutional amendments being proposed at the time, wrote in favor of the Seventh Amendment. In his series of essays, the *Letters of Centinel* (1787–1788), he argued that judges often had "a bias towards those of their own rank and dignity; for it is not to be expected, that the few should be attentive to the rights of the many." Bryan praised the amendment because it "preserves in the hands of the people, that share which they ought to have in the administration of justice, and prevents the encroachments of the more powerful and wealthy citizens."

The Seventh Amendment and Common Law

The Seventh Amendment states that:

> In Suits at common law, where the value in controversy shall exceed twenty dollars, the right of trial by jury shall be preserved, and no fact tried by a jury shall be otherwise re-examined in any Court of the United States, than according to the rules of the common law.

It is important to understand why the framers of the Bill of Rights based the Seventh Amendment on common-law practices. After all, common-law practices were once a source of corruption in England and controversy and unfairness in the American colonies. However, by relying upon common-law precedent, a judge is less likely to come up with a sentence, or punishment, that is unreasonable and not appropriate to the case. For example, if a judge sentences someone to a $100 fine to settle a property line dispute, common law would ensure that the next person to be sentenced in a similar dispute would not be arbitrarily fined $1,000 or have his or her property seized. Instead, a reasonable fine similar to that imposed in the earlier case would be imposed in the current case.

The Seventh Amendment also separates the roles of the judge and jury. The jury decides whether a party is guilty, and the judge decides the appropriate punishment in the case if a guilty verdict is reached. If either the judge or jury decided both guilt and punishment, there would be much more opportunity for unjust rulings and unjust sentencing. This way a jury that has found someone guilty cannot impose an overly harsh or overly lenient penalty. Instead, a judge imposes the penalty and must follow certain guidelines in doing so. And a person who has been brought to court cannot be found guilty by only one person. A guilty verdict requires a unanimous vote of twelve people. This ensures that the evidence must be strong and convincing.

The jury has to worry only about hearing the arguments and weighing the evidence in the case. If the evidence argues for a guilty verdict, then they must deliver one, regardless of who the accused is and how powerful or wealthy he or she may be. Similarly, the judge is not able to let his or her opinions or political views enter the case, and he or she can't argue for the jury to come to a particular decision. The judge can only impose penalties upon people deemed guilty by the jury.

CHAPTER TWO

THE EVOLUTION OF THE SEVENTH AMENDMENT

The Seventh Amendment was ratified in 1791 as one of the original ten amendments to the U.S. Constitution, known collectively as the Bill of Rights. Compared to many of the other amendments in the Bill of Rights, the Seventh Amendment was passed with little controversy and with little opposition. It was not until many years after the amendment was passed that changes were made to it.

Fine-Tuning the Seventh Amendment

In 1872, it was decided by the U.S. Supreme Court that the parties involved in a civil case—the plaintiff and defendant—may decide that

The Seventh Amendment helped David Goldman win a five-year custody battle for his son Sean. When Sean's parents divorced, he was taken to Brazil with his mother, who remarried there. After she died, Goldman had to fight for years to regain custody of his son.

they do not want a jury to decide their case. Instead, they may opt for a judge to solve their dispute for them. Today, judges do indeed make the decisions in many civil cases involving family law and child custody, without the help of a jury.

Yet many civil cases are still decided by a jury. In 1899, the Supreme Court decided that civil case juries would be made up of twelve members. Today, trials may have between six and twelve members on a jury, depending on the laws of the state in which the case is being tried.

In 1900, an important Supreme Court decision was made regarding jury decisions in civil cases. It stated that a unanimous decision must be reached by the jury. In other words, all jury members must agree on the guilty or not guilty verdict. Failure to reach a unanimous decision would result in what is called a hung jury. The judge would be forced to declare a mistrial if further jury deliberations did not lead to a unanimous vote. The judge would then order the case to be retried in the future with a new jury in place.

One of the most important decisions regarding the Seventh Amendment occurred in 1970. This is when the Supreme Court confirmed that corporations should be able to have the same protection under the Seventh Amendment that private citizens do. This ruling had some major consequences for individuals as well as corporations.

This protection under the Seventh Amendment was actually intended for the corporation's shareholders. These are individuals who own small shares, or portions, of the company. When someone buys stock in a company, he or she is buying shares in its ownership. The person's money helps fund the company's operations. Shareholders are average citizens. So when cases are brought against corporations, or in other words its shareholders, the Supreme Court decided that they should be able to have their interests protected just as any other citizen would. In many cases, individual shareholders own very small portions of a company. They have very little chance to have their voices heard, therefore, and have little influence over the decision-making process of the corporation's directors.

In a case involving the investment company Lehman Corporation, the Supreme Court upheld the right of Lehman shareholders to sue, on behalf of the corporation, Lehman's managers, whom they accused of poor and harmful business practices.

The Supreme Court decision resulting from the Lehman Corporation case confirmed the shareholders' right to a jury trial. This, in turn, allowed shareholders to both sue on behalf of their corporation and defend their corporation against lawsuits (lawsuits are civil cases in which a plaintiff sues a defendant). It also allowed shareholders to sue the corporation's managers if their actions harm the corporation and the interests of its shareholders through misconduct, bad faith, negligence, or other forms of corporate mismanagement.

Corporate Law

As a result of allowing corporations the right to jury trials and protection under the Seventh Amendment, all large companies now have their own teams of lawyers working on their behalf and in the best interests of their shareholders. This makes the playing field a bit uneven when an individual sues or is sued by a company. Not many average citizens can

These plaintiffs are lined up at the U.S. Supreme Court Building to hear public arguments against a cigarette company in a class-action lawsuit. The plaintiffs claimed they were misled into thinking that "low tar" and "light" cigarettes were a healthier smoking alternative.

afford the many hours of legal advice and attorney protection required during a civil legal proceeding. But most corporations can afford to go to great lengths to protect their interests. They have far more money at their disposal and can endure lengthy legal proceedings that will quickly bankrupt the individual opposing them in court.

In some cases, the best interests of a corporation do not benefit the public or the consumer. When companies are sued, it is often over misuse of money or issues of health or safety. Fortunately, impartial juries are unswayed by a corporation's enormous wealth, power, or influence. They listen to the case in court and carefully weigh the evidence that leads to a fair and just decision about whether a party is guilty or not guilty. A jury should be immune from bribes, intimidation, and other forms of influence peddling that the wealthy and powerful may attempt to use. The members of the jury must render a fair verdict based only on the evidence presented to them.

Selecting a Jury

All American citizens over the age of eighteen can be called for jury duty. The names of jury candidates are often pulled from voting records. The court cases on which they serve can be on the county or state level. Jurors report to a courthouse on a designated day and the process of choosing jurors begins.

Prospective jurors often wait for hours to be called upon at random to be considered for a case. At that time, the prospective jurors meet with the attorneys, the judge, and sometimes the plaintiff or defendant in the case. The lawyers ask the jurors questions to determine whether they have prior knowledge of the case and if they have already formed an opinion on the defendant's guilt or innocence. If a juror has heard any details of the case before and formed an opinion, or if the juror knows one of the people involved in the case, he or she will not be chosen to be a juror. If a prospective juror feels he or she cannot be impartial because of a particular issue raised by the case, he or she will explain the problem to the judge and attorneys. The judge and lawyers will then decide whether the person should be removed from the jury pool.

It can sometimes take days to select a jury that attorneys from both sides of the dispute can accept. That is why courts call a large number of prospective jurors together at one time so that there are plenty of people to choose from in a case.

What Does a Juror Do?

The job of a juror is to listen carefully to all of the evidence being presented in a case. The attorneys for both the plaintiff and the defendant will present the case and all of its evidence to the jury. The jurors are instructed to be impartial and not to take sides in the debate or let their own experiences or opinions get in the way of the decision they are trying to make. They must not let the character of the people in the case cloud their judgment. They are instructed to judge only whether a party is guilty or not guilty of a particular claim, not whether they seem like good or bad people or honest or deceitful.

Based on the evidence before them, all a jury must decide is whether the person, persons, or corporation did what the plaintiff claims they did and if that was against the law or constituted fault or wrongdoing. They cannot find someone guilty of something he or she has not been charged with. They cannot find someone guilty because they "feel," "sense," "suspect," or "strongly believe" the person is guilty. The available evidence must prove "beyond a reasonable doubt" that a party is guilty or not guilty.

Jurors must also listen carefully to the testimony, or formal statement, given by people who are questioned by the attorneys in the case. Testimonies often include details provided by witnesses who saw a

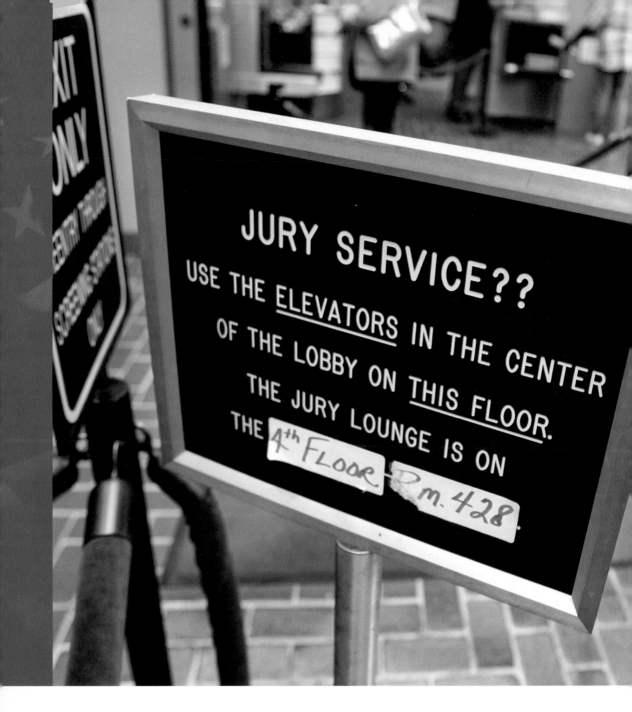

dispute occur or who have unique "insider" information about the incidents at the center of the case.

After jurors have heard every piece of evidence in the case, they are asked to discuss the case together in private chambers. One juror is

Citizens have a right to a fair trial by jury, and they also have a related responsibility and obligation to report for jury duty when summoned and to serve on a jury if chosen.

often named the foreman. This person has the job of leading the jurors in discussion and asking the important questions that will help the jurors examine and draw conclusions about the evidence. He or she also asks the judge for clarifications of his or her instructions or points of law and for rereading of important testimony. The foreman organizes votes among the jurors to see where everyone stands, resolves disputes among jurors, and, once a unanimous verdict has been reached, announces that verdict in the courtroom.

Being a juror is one of the most important duties we have as Americans. The decisions of a jury have profound consequences for all the parties involved. Jurors take this responsibility seriously, and the system works remarkably well because of it. In complicated cases, the jury may have to sit on a case for months, missing work and other obligations in the meantime. In the case of civil lawsuits, as opposed to criminal trials, the juries will probably not have to stay sequestered, or isolated. Sequestration is when jurors are kept apart from other people (including their family members) in hotel rooms when the trial is adjourned (out of session) at day's end. However, in some high-profile civil and criminal cases, the juries may be asked to stay in hotels and away from the public while the case is being tried.

This is sometimes for their protection. In rare and extreme instances, associates of the defendant might try to bribe, threaten, or harm jurors. Sometimes sequestration is used to keep the jurors from encountering media coverage of the event that will possibly sway their decision.

In all cases, jurors are instructed to not talk about the case to anyone. The opinions of people outside the courtroom who have not heard all of the evidence from both sides in the case may possibly sway the jurors' decision. That decision would be tainted since it had not been arrived at by a thorough weighing of all the evidence. It may be difficult sometimes for jurors to keep the details of the case completely private, especially when at home with family members. But it is important to the judicial process that the case be decided by the jury and only by the jury.

Avoiding Jury Bias

Attorneys on both sides of a dispute work hard to pick jury members who do not have certain experiences or opinions that might make them far more inclined to vote one way or another in a civil case. For instance, someone who has been a victim of identify theft might not be chosen for a case centering on that crime. Such a jury member will have experienced the same hardships as the alleged victim, and this will likely make him or her feel sympathetic to the plaintiff. On the other hand, lawyers for the plaintiff would not want to choose an entire jury of people who have never heard of what identity theft is. Such a jury would not have the experience necessary to understand the suffering the incident has caused the victim.

Juries are routinely chosen so that they are roughly half male and half female. Ideally, jury members will come from varied economic, ethnic, and social backgrounds. This makes a well-rounded jury with vast life experiences to draw upon when deciding a civil case. A diverse jury helps guarantee that not all members will think alike. It also helps ensure that, as a group, the jury won't be either overly sympathetic with or hostile to a plaintiff or defendant of a particular ethnic, racial, gender, religious, or economic background.

The Jury's Decision Is Final

Part of the Seventh Amendment guarantees that once a jury has reached its verdict, the decision is final. The only time a judge can decide that a jury's decision should be disregarded is when the judge feels that the jury did not consider all of the evidence in the case or did not act fairly when considering the facts. If this is the case, the judge can ask that the ruling be thrown out and the case be retried at another time with another jury.

When the plaintiff or defendant is unhappy with the ruling of a case, the only thing he or she can do to try to change the decision is to ask for an appeal. In an appeal, a higher court is requested to review the case, the legal arguments made during it, the evidence presented, the judge's conduct of the proceedings, and the jury's deliberations and decision. Whoever has brought the appeal hopes that the lower court's decision will be overturned. In some cases, an appeals process may reach all the way to the Supreme Court. The Supreme Court justices are then asked to make a final and definitive judgment in the case. They will either uphold or overturn the various lower courts' rulings on the matter.

CHAPTER THREE

LAWSUITS AND OVERCROWDED COURTS

The right to have a jury decide one's fate or solve a dispute is comforting to many Americans. They trust that a group of impartial citizens—peers similar to themselves—would likely make a fair and honest decision in the courtroom. So what are the possible drawbacks to the Seventh Amendment in today's society? It's not the juries themselves that are a problem; it's the sheer number of lawsuits being filed in the United States. There are more lawsuits filed and more trial lawyers in the United States than in any other country in the world. This puts a strain on the entire legal system and may result in cases not receiving the attention and care they deserve. It can also result in the filing of frivolous lawsuits that have little or no merit.

Setting Precedents

When cases are decided in court, precedents are set that help juries as well as judges make decisions in similar cases in the future. Older cases provide basic guidelines for what circumstances make someone guilty or liable for damages and what those damages should be. For example, drunk driving cases are quite often decided in favor of the innocent victims who were injured. As long as there is proof that the driver was intoxicated and at fault, the biggest decision in the court case would be exactly how much money should be granted to the plaintiff.

Based on legal precedent (the results of earlier similar cases), the costs of the victim's medical expenses are typically granted in the award. The victim often also receives money typically referred to as damages or pain and suffering. This means that the person's emotional and psychological damages are deserving of compensation. Juries typically declare that any lost income the victim suffered because of the accident would also require compensation from the defendant.

Lawsuits: The American Way

People sue each other for a wide range of reasons. A person might sue a neighbor over a property line dispute if he thinks the neighbor is encroaching on his land. Another person might sue someone if she was bitten by the person's dog or if she believes that something was stolen from her. And the lawsuits don't stop there. People sue corporations for selling them defective products or foods that make them sick or unhealthy. It may sound like "the American Way" to stand up for oneself in a dispute. There is nothing wrong with seeking justice when someone has been wronged, mistreated, cheated, or harmed. But the increase in lawsuits has had some negative effects on the justice system.

Why do people sue each other instead of trying to work out a dispute on their own? One reason is that they want to win as much money as possible from the outcome of the case. They are hoping a jury will decide in their favor and award them a large amount in cash damages.

Americans have long been fascinated with the legal system, as demonstrated by the many television shows and movies that center upon courtroom drama. Judge Judy Sheindlin (*left*) is the star of a popular court show called *Judge Judy*.

However, is the search for money the best reason to burden the American legal system with a time-consuming, labor-intensive, and very expensive court case? A frivolous lawsuit is one that does not have a legitimate legal reason to be brought forth. Generally, frivolous lawsuits are mere attempts at "cash grabs" or an effort to discredit an enemy. It has been argued that there are so many frivolous lawsuits clogging American courts that there should be laws passed to prevent them.

The American legal system is set up in a way that may encourage more lawsuits than are typical in other countries. In the United States, each party that is being sued must pay for his or her own legal protection. In other countries, especially in Europe, the court costs and legal fees of both parties are paid by the party that loses the case. This possibility might keep someone from initiating a case against someone else if he or she considered how much money would have to be spent in the event of an unsuccessful outcome in court. Plaintiffs would have to be very sure they could win the case before they set the legal wheels in motion.

In the United States, however, where there is no such check on people's willingness to bring lawsuits, the number of civil cases continues to rise. The highest increase in these cases has been against doctors and the health care industry.

Doctors and Lawsuits

When someone goes to the doctor's office or hospital, he or she expects good care and trusts the doctor with his or her health. So when something does not go as expected, that person may feel that the doctor's care or the doctor's diagnosis was to blame. The patient may feel like he or she wants to sue, to win damages that will help pay for medical expenses or cover the costs of any disability or therapy that may be necessary. Sometimes patients just want to make someone pay for an honest mistake that was made. Other times, a doctor may be clearly at fault and may have committed malpractice. Malpractice is poor medical care that goes beyond an honest mistake into questionable and incompetent conduct.

There have been so many legal cases against doctors that they often feel that concern over lawsuits interferes with their work. Seventy-nine percent of doctors admit that they have second-guessed their own professional judgment about what is wrong with a patient. As a result, they have ordered additional expensive tests that they would not normally have ordered just because they feared that they could be sued if their diagnosis was incorrect. These additional, and sometimes unnecessary, tests increase the cost of health care for patients. The rising cost of health care is affected by the number of lawsuits against doctors. In addition to more expensive tests, doctors and/or their hospitals are forced to carry very costly malpractice insurance. The American Medical Association (AMA) has tried to limit the number of malpractice lawsuits against doctors. It feels that the constant threat of lawsuits negatively affects the quality of health care as well as its cost.

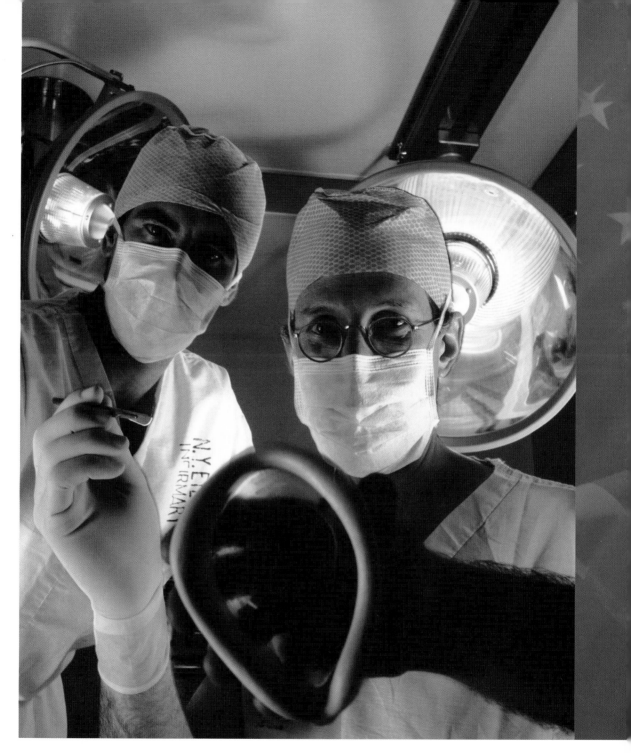

The medical industry has the highest rate of malpractice lawsuits of any industry. This affects medical costs, insurance prices, and often a doctor's ability to perform his or her job properly and effectively.

Lawsuits also interfere with the doctor's ability to take care of his or her patients. Being sued is a time-consuming process. When lawsuits are brought against doctors, the accused cannot ignore it if they want to defend themselves and protect their reputations and livelihood. The legal process is expensive and demands a lot of preparation time with a lawyer to gather all of the necessary information that would prove the doctor's innocence. This distracting, anxiety-inducing, and time-consuming process can take away from a doctor's ability to perform his or her job.

Doctors and surgeons are frequently sued for incorrect diagnoses, unsafe care, and even wrongful death. Honest mistakes in the doctor's office or operating room can be costly if the patient is negatively affected and decides to sue.

How to Survive Being Sued

The average citizen may have even more trouble if he or she is sued than a doctor would. Lawyer fees are high. Not everyone has a doctor's salary or the backing of a major hospital and may not be able to afford a talented lawyer who will provide good legal advice and a strong defense in court. It is not a requirement that someone

Despite the expense, average citizens facing legal difficulties may benefit greatly by seeking a lawyer's advice and hiring a lawyer to represent them during a lawsuit. Organizations like the Legal Aid Society offer legal services and representation to low-income clients.

who is being sued hire a lawyer. But the defendant may have a much better chance at proving his or her innocence if someone with extensive law training takes on the case. When people decide to defend themselves in court without the expert help and guidance of a lawyer, they

may be missing out on the detailed knowledge of many laws, precedents, strategies, and loopholes that might help their case and establish their innocence.

There are a few options for someone who cannot hire a lawyer and does not have the necessary legal knowledge to defend himself or herself in court. Occasionally, claims made against a person may be covered by his or her insurance, such as in cases involving car accidents and accidents that occur in someone's home.

Another option is to settle out of court. This means that the plaintiff and the defendant must come to an agreement on their own about any money or other settlement that the defendant will agree to pay the plaintiff in exchange for not having to go to court. This settlement usually proves to be less expensive than engaging in the lawsuit process.

A third option is to default the case, or simply ignore the charges. In that case, the defendant will still owe the plaintiff the money he or she has requested in the lawsuit, but the defendant will be spared the legal fees that would have been charged and the time it would have taken to try the case. This would be similar to pleading guilty to the charges, because the other side will be considered the winner in the case. But in a case of default, the court does not have to convene, a jury does not have to be chosen, and lawyers do not have to be retained for weeks on end.

Crowding in the Court

The high number of lawsuits in the United States means that courthouses are overcrowded with cases to try and juries to select. Both parties involved in a lawsuit may end up waiting for a long time before their court case even gets underway. As a result of these delays, more parties are likely to settle out of court.

While settling helps ease congestion in the courts, it can also sometimes mean that a guilty party will not suffer the full consequences of his or her actions. If a guilty person simply agrees to pay money to another party to compensate for his or her actions, he or she may not face a severe enough penalty. As a result, the person may not feel as powerful a disincentive to avoid similar trouble in the future. When cases are settled out of court, the justice system is not helping to correct the misbehavior of citizens who would normally receive some sort of penalty from a judge if a jury finds them guilty or liable.

CHAPTER FOUR

THE SEVENTH AMENDMENT GOES TO WORK

Even though more lawsuits (many of them frivolous) are filed in the United States than in any other country in the world, there may well be a good reason for this. The founding document of the United States—the Constitution—protects the rights of American citizens. Any local, state, or federal law must respect those same rights or be declared unconstitutional by the Supreme Court. One of these constitutional rights is the right to bring a civil case against someone and sue for damages.

Suppose someone is injured in a car accident caused by a drunk driver. That driver was not following the law. By breaking the law, he or she endangered the lives of other drivers on the road and injured an innocent person. In the United States, the injured party can seek compensation for the harm caused by the person's negligent and illegal actions. The injured party has the right to sue that person, and a jury will hear the case and decide who is at fault and what the compensation should be. For example, the victim may receive money for his or her hardship. This money may have to be used for the medical bills that have piled up as a result of the accident and any medical care that will be required in the future due to the injury.

The Seventh Amendment has done a lot of good for many people. Civil trials decided by an impartial jury help settle disputes fairly. And the outcomes of the cases sometimes encourage corporations to change their harmful policies and improve their operations. Sometimes these policy changes improve public health, for example. These changes may never have been made without a lawsuit being brought to force the problem out into the open. In one such case, a lawsuit against a company resulted in policy and operational changes that actually saved people's lives.

The Case of Pacific Gas and Electric Company

The Pacific Gas and Electric Company, or PG&E, is a utility that provides electricity and natural gas to about two-thirds of California. Natural gas is not something that the company gets locally. Instead, it is delivered through underground pipelines from Texas. In order for the gas to travel so far, it must be repressurized approximately every 300 miles (483 kilometers) at designated stations.

One of these pressurization stations was located in the town of Hinkley, California. PG&E must use chemicals at the treatment sites to make sure the repressurization works correctly. One particular chemical, hexavalent chromium, was used in water-cooling towers to prevent the development of rust inside the towers. This chemical seeped out of the water-cooling towers and into the soil and groundwater, contaminating Hinkley's drinking water and sickening townspeople.

Over time, cases of organ failure, birth defects, and cancer increased in the area. These disease clusters were eventually linked to

the chemical found in the drinking water. A lawsuit against PG&E led to many arguments in court as well as arbitration. Arbitration is a faster and more streamlined way plaintiffs and defendants may work to resolve disputes outside of the courtroom. Together they appoint an

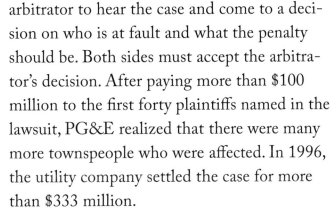

arbitrator to hear the case and come to a decision on who is at fault and what the penalty should be. Both sides must accept the arbitrator's decision. After paying more than $100 million to the first forty plaintiffs named in the lawsuit, PG&E realized that there were many more townspeople who were affected. In 1996, the utility company settled the case for more than $333 million.

After the water contamination was corrected by PG&E, the problem was far from over regarding the people the chemical affected. Hexavalent chromium is toxic and causes cancers and birth defects. These problems take time to develop in the body. The number of people affected by the tainted water continued to rise even after the suit was settled. In 2006, an additional $315 million was paid to more victims by PG&E, and another $20 million was given in 2008.

The problem with Hinkley's drinking water was first uncovered by a law office clerk named

In Hinkley, California, three children read a sign across the street from their home that warns of polluted water. This pollution is still affecting the residents of the town thirty years after a dangerous chemical used by gas company PG&E seeped into the town's drinking water.

Erin Brockovich. She researched the cases that came through the law office and was able to slowly discover what connected them all and what was happening. The 2000 movie *Erin Brockovich*, starring Julia Roberts, is about the PG&E case.

Evidence Tampering

When a court case is being prepared, lawyers from both sides gather evidence that can prove the truth of the plaintiff's complaint or establish

the defendant's guilt or innocence. Evidence is a very important part of a trial. Evidence might include paperwork and correspondence passed between the two parties, personal property of someone in the case, and even eyewitness testimonies offered on the witness stand in court.

Sometimes, in trying to cover up their guilt in a situation, a person might forge or destroy documents, dispose of any material or objects that are incriminating, or even ask a witness to lie on the stand. These kinds of activities are known as tampering with evidence, and it is a crime. Once evidence has been submitted in a case, it is held by the court and neither party is allowed to handle it during the trial. The consequences for tampering with evidence can be jail time, probation, or community service, depending on how severe and damaging the tampering incident was. When cases of evidence tampering are discovered, the trial process may have to be repeated in a new venue, possibly with a new jury and judge.

A security guard at a federal courthouse in San Diego, California, helps a lawyer deliver boxes of documents relating to lawsuits brought against the automaker Toyota. The cases all involve a sudden acceleration problem in Toyota cars that resulted in accidents, injuries, and several deaths.

The Case Against Toyota

Another example of the outcome of civil lawsuits providing benefits to the general public is the November 2009 class action lawsuit brought against the carmaker Toyota. A class action lawsuit is a type of civil case in which many people, usually consumers, are involved in a single complaint against a company. In this case, more than two thousand Toyota owners claimed that their cars experienced sudden unintended acceleration problems. While driving at normal speeds, the plaintiffs in the lawsuit claimed that their cars suddenly and uncontrollably accelerated to top speeds, and the drivers were unable to make the cars stop. The problem was traced back to a defective electronic throttle system.

The Seventh Amendment in Action

Whenever a jury makes a decision in a civil case, the Seventh Amendment can be observed in action. The amendment is put to use every day in courthouses across the country. The decisions have a great impact on people's lives. There are many examples of cases that demonstrate the wisdom and fairness of a jury. One such example shows the way that justice can be served when twelve people gather to sort through evidence, evaluate arguments, and come to a clear-eyed decision about what happened, who is at fault, and what a reasonable penalty should be.

In 2006, carpenter Luis Barros fell 15 feet (4.5 meters) at a construction site. Barros sued the construction company he worked for because he suffered serious injuries to his spine and ankle. The construction crew was renovating a high-rise condominium in New Rochelle, New York. In the course of the workday, the construction crew often had to move between platforms and scaffolds set up on the outside of the building.

While moving between a platform and scaffold, the carpenter fell. Barros spent two days in the hospital and claimed that his injuries prevented him from performing basic everyday tasks. He had a lot of pain from the injury and had several surgeries to correct disc and bone problems later on. He was also unable to work on future construction sites due to his injuries.

Claiming the scaffold was structurally defective, Barros sued the general contractor of the project for not providing the correct safety equipment. He also sued the owner of the premises for not providing the safe working conditions required under state labor laws. Barros sued for a total of $18.5 million, which included payment for his past, present, and future pain and suffering, as well as for lost income and medical costs.

The defense in the case claimed that the carpenter should have been more careful in the way that he moved between platforms, that his physical condition was not very good before the accident, and that he was exaggerating his injuries.

The jury heard the case and was presented with evidence, including eyewitness testimonies and expert medical opinions. However, after careful consideration of this evidence, the jury decided that some of Barros's injuries were likely caused by pre-existing physical problems. So while the jury found that the plaintiff did deserve to receive money in the case, the amount of the damages received was reduced from $18.5 million to $8 million.

This jury did an exceptional job of sifting through the evidence, weighing the validity of opposing and contradictory arguments, and arriving at a judgment that was evenhanded and fair to both parties. Each case that goes before a jury is different, and each one must be examined carefully by the jury to make sure the judgment will be fair. The Seventh Amendment guarantees that right to all Americans.

The faulty throttle caused Toyota to issue widespread recalls of many of its vehicles so the problem could be fixed. The plaintiffs' lawsuit claimed that more than two hundred injuries and sixteen deaths resulted from this car part defect.

Doing the Right Thing, Thanks to the Seventh Amendment

As both the Toyota and Pacific Electric and Gas cases show, lawsuits against companies (and individuals) can cause enormous harm to their reputations. When legitimate lawsuits are filed by people harmed by a company's actions or products, the general public tends to lose trust in the companies. Whether or not the lawsuit is successful for the plaintiffs, the bad publicity often forces the companies being sued to take actions to reform their policies, fix dangerous problems, and compensate those who were harmed.

Whether the problems that give rise to lawsuits are intentional or accidental, the public has the right to protect themselves against dangerous and unhealthful situations. They have the right to sue the parties responsible for inflicting harm or doing wrong. They have the right to have their complaints heard and decided upon by a jury of peers. And they have the right to receive compensation for damages and suffering if a jury finds in their favor. All of these rights are granted and guaranteed to them by the Seventh Amendment to the U.S. Constitution.

In 2004, an arthritis medication called Vioxx was removed from the U.S. market because of its role in causing heart attacks in some patients. At left, a company spokesperson talks to the media after a jury awarded $253 million to the widow of a Vioxx user who died of a heart attack.

AMENDMENTS
TO THE U.S. CONSTITUTION

First Amendment (proposed 1789; ratified 1791): Freedom of religion, speech, press, assembly, and petition

Second Amendment (proposed 1789; ratified 1791): Right to bear arms

Third Amendment (proposed 1789; ratified 1791): No quartering of soldiers in private houses in times of peace

Fourth Amendment (proposed 1789; ratified 1791): Interdiction of unreasonable search and seizure; requirement of search warrants

Fifth Amendment (proposed 1789; ratified 1791): Indictments; due process; self-incrimination; double jeopardy; eminent domain

Sixth Amendment (proposed 1789; ratified 1791): Right to a fair and speedy public trial; notice of accusations; confronting one's accuser; subpoenas; right to counsel

Seventh Amendment (proposed 1789; ratified 1791): Right to a trial by jury in civil cases

Eighth Amendment (proposed 1789; ratified 1791): No excessive bail and fines; no cruel or unusual punishment

Ninth Amendment (proposed 1789; ratified 1791): Protection of unenumerated rights (rights inferred from other legal rights but that are not themselves coded or enumerated in written constitution and laws)

Tenth Amendment (proposed 1789; ratified 1791): Limits the power of the federal government

Eleventh Amendment (proposed 1794; ratified 1795): Sovereign immunity (immunity of states from suits brought by out-of-state citizens and foreigners living outside of state's borders)

Twelfth Amendment (proposed 1803; ratified 1804): Revision of presidential election procedures (electoral college)

Thirteenth Amendment (proposed 1865; ratified 1865): Abolition of slavery

Fourteenth Amendment (proposed 1866; ratified 1868): Citizenship; state due process; application of Bill of Rights to states; revision to apportionment of congressional representatives; denies public office to anyone who has rebelled against the United States

Fifteenth Amendment (proposed 1869; ratified 1870): Suffrage no longer restricted by race

Sixteenth Amendment (proposed 1909; ratified 1913): Allows federal income tax

Seventeenth Amendment (proposed 1912; ratified 1913): Direct election to the U.S. Senate by popular vote

Eighteenth Amendment (proposed 1917; ratified 1919): Prohibition of alcohol

Nineteenth Amendment (proposed 1919; ratified 1920): Women's suffrage

Twentieth Amendment (proposed 1932; ratified 1933): Term commencement for Congress (January 3) and president (January 20)

Twenty-first Amendment (proposed 1933; ratified 1933): Repeal of Eighteenth Amendment (Prohibition)

Twenty-second Amendment (proposed 1947; ratified 1951): Limits president to two terms

Twenty-third Amendment (proposed 1960; ratified 1961): Representation of District of Columbia in electoral college

Twenty-fourth Amendment (proposed 1962; ratified 1964): Prohibition of restriction of voting rights due to nonpayment of poll taxes

Twenty-fifth Amendment (proposed 1965; ratified 1967): Presidential succession

Twenty-sixth Amendment (proposed 1971; ratified 1971): Voting age of eighteen

Twenty-seventh Amendment (proposed 1789; ratified 1992): Congressional compensation

Proposed but Unratified Amendments

Congressional Apportionment Amendment (proposed 1789; still technically pending): Apportionment of U.S. representatives

Titles of Nobility Amendment (proposed 1810; still technically pending): Prohibition of titles of nobility

Corwin Amendment (proposed 1861; still technically pending, though superseded by Thirteenth Amendment): Preservation of slavery

Child Labor Amendment (proposed 1924; still technically pending): Congressional power to regulate child labor

Equal Rights Amendment (proposed 1972; expired): Prohibition of inequality of men and women

District of Columbia Voting Rights Amendment (proposed 1978; expired): District of Columbia voting rights

GLOSSARY

Anti-Federalist A member of a political movement in early America who wanted states to have more power than the federal government.

appeal To apply to a higher court to review and reverse a lower court's decision.

arbitration The process of reaching a judgment or settling a dispute outside of a court.

Bill of Rights The first ten amendments to the U.S. Constitution that outline the various rights and powers of the federal government, the states, and the individual citizen.

civil law A system of law regarding private disputes, rather than criminal activity.

class action A lawsuit filed on behalf of a large group of people.

common law A system of law developed by judges through decisions in courts, rather than laws created by the legislative (Congress) or executive (president) branches of government.

defendant The person in a lawsuit who is accused of having done something unfair, harmful, or damaging.

due process Fair treatment under the law.

foreman The person who represents and speaks for a jury.

impartial Completely fair, objective, and evenhanded in judgment.

jury A group of citizens assigned to make an honest and objective ruling in a court case.

magistrate Officer, judge, or official who judges cases.

mistrial A trial that is declared invalid because of errors in the proceedings.

plaintiff A person who brings a legal case against someone else in a court of law.

precedent An earlier event, action, decision, or outcome that guides decisions in similar present and future situations.

ratify To confirm or approve something; to agree upon a proposed law and sign it.

sequestered Hidden away; kept separate and apart; isolated.

shareholder A person who owns shares in a public company.

testimony A formal statement, such as one given in court.

unanimous In full agreement, with no dissent or disagreement.

FOR MORE INFORMATION

American Bar Association (ABA)
321 North Clark Street
Chicago, IL 60654-7598
(312) 988-5000
Web site: http://www.abanet.org
The ABA is the national representative of the legal profession. Its mission is to serve its members (lawyers and judges) and the public by defending liberty and delivering justice.

American Civil Liberties Union (ACLU)
125 Broad Street, 18th Floor
New York, NY 10004
(212) 549-2500
Web site: http://www.aclu.org
The ACLU views itself as the nation's guardian of liberty. It works daily in courts, legislatures, and communities to defend and preserve the individual rights and liberties that the Constitution and laws of the United States guarantee everyone in the United States. These rights include free speech, freedom of the press, freedom of association and assembly, freedom of religion, freedom from discrimination, the right to due process, and the right to privacy.

American Law Institute
4025 Chestnut Street
Philadelphia, PA 19104
(215) 243-1600
Web site: http://www.ali.org

The American Law Institute is one of the leading independent legal organizations in the United States. It produces scholarly work to clarify, modernize, and otherwise improve the law. The institute (made up of four thousand highly accomplished and respected lawyers, judges, and law professors) drafts, discusses, revises, and publishes Restatements of the Law, model statutes, and principles of law that exert a strong influence on courts and legislatures, legal scholarship, and legal education.

Harvard Law Review

Gannett House
1511 Massachusetts Avenue
Cambridge, MA 02138
(617) 495-7889
Web site: http://www.harvardlawreview.org

The *Harvard Law Review* is an important academic forum for legal scholarship. It is designed to be an effective research tool for practicing lawyers and students of the law. The *Review* publishes articles by professors, judges, and lawyers and solicits reviews of important recent books from recognized experts.

Harvard Law School

1563 Massachusetts Avenue
Cambridge, MA 02138
(617) 495-3100
Web site: http://www.law.harvard.edu

Harvard Law School is one of the nation's leading law schools, featuring a diverse faculty of broad experience, expertise, and legal knowledge and a student body that comes from every state in the United States and more than seventy countries. The school offers more than 260 courses and seminars that cover a broad range of traditional and emerging legal fields. The law school community also hosts numerous research programs and publications, including books, scholarly periodicals, newsletters, and a weekly student newspaper.

Legal Aid Society
199 Water Street
New York, NY 10038
(212) 577-3346
Web site: http://www.legal-aid.org
The Legal Aid Society is the nation's oldest and largest provider of legal services to those who cannot afford to hire a lawyer. Founded in 1876, the society provides a full range of civil legal services, as well as criminal defense work and juvenile rights representation in family court.

National Archives and Records Administration (NARA)
8601 Adelphi Road
College Park, MD 20740-6001
Web site: http://www.archives.gov
The NARA is the nation's record keeper. The archives house the Declaration of Independence, the Articles of Confederation, the Constitution, the Bill of Rights, the Emancipation Proclamation, and the Louisiana Purchase agreement, along with other documents of national importance like military and immigration records, and even the *Apollo 11* flight plan. Archives locations in fourteen cities, from coast to coast, protect and provide public access to millions of records.

Supreme Court of the United States
1 First Street NE
Washington, DC 20543
(202) 479-3000
Web site: http://www.supremecourt.gov
The Supreme Court of the United States is the highest judicial body in the country and leads the federal judiciary. It consists of the chief justice of the United States and eight associate justices who are nominated by the president and confirmed by a majority vote of the Senate. Once appointed, justices can serve for life. Their time on the court ends only upon death, resignation, retirement, or conviction on

impeachment charges. The court meets in Washington, D.C., in the U.S. Supreme Court Building. The Supreme Court primarily hears appeals of lower court decisions.

Web Sites

Due to the changing nature of Internet links, Rosen Publishing has developed an online list of Web sites related to the subject of this book. This site is updated regularly. Please use this link to access the list:

http://www.rosenlinks.com/ausc/7th

FOR FURTHER READING

Burgan, Michael. *The Creation of the U.S. Constitution* (Graphic History). Mankato, MN: Capstone Press, 2007.

Cheney, Lynn, and Greg Harlin. *We the People: The Story of Our Constitution*. New York, NY: Simon & Schuster Children's Publishing, 2008.

Coleman, Wim, and Pat Perrin, eds. *The Constitution and the Bill of Rights*. Auburndale, MA: History Compass, 2006.

Finkelman, Paul. *American Documents: The Constitution*. Des Moines, IA: National Geographic Children's Books, 2005.

Fradin, Dennis Brindell. *The Bill of Rights* (Turning Points in U.S. History). Tarrytown, NY: Marshall Cavendish Children's Books, 2008.

Fradin, Dennis Brindell. *The Founders: The 39 Stories Behind the U.S. Constitution*. New York, NY: Walker Books for Young Readers, 2005.

Isaacs, Sally Senzell. *Understanding the Bill of Rights* (Documenting Early America). New York, NY: Crabtree Publishing Co., 2008.

Isaacs, Sally Senzell. *Understanding the U.S. Constitution* (Documenting Early America). New York, NY: Crabtree Publishing Co., 2008.

JusticeLearning.org. *The United States Constitution: What It Says, What It Means: A Hip Pocket Guide*. New York, NY: Oxford University Press, 2005.

Leavitt, Amie J. *The Bill of Rights in Translation: What It Really Means*. Mankato, MN: Capstone Press, 2008.

Manatt, Kathleen G. *Law and Order*. Ann Arbor, MI: Cherry Lake Publishing, 2007.

Pederson, Charles E. *The U.S. Constitution and Bill of Rights*. Edina, MN: ABDO Publishing, 2010.

Ransom, Candice F. *Who Wrote the U.S. Constitution and Other Questions About the Constitutional Convention of 1787*. Minneapolis, MN: Lerner Classroom, 2010.

Smith, Rich. *Seventh Amendment: The Right to a Trial by Jury*. Edina, MN: ABDO Publishing, 2007.

Sobel, Syl. *The Bill of Rights: Protecting Our Freedom Then and Now*. Hauppauge, NY: Barron's Educational Series, 2008.

Taylor-Butler Christine. *The Bill of Rights* (True Books). New York, NY: Children's Press, 2008.

Taylor-Butler, Christine. *The Constitution of the United States* (True Books). New York, NY: Children's Press, 2008.

Taylor-Butler, Christine. *The Supreme Court* (True Books). New York, NY: Children's Press, 2008.

Yero, Judith Lloyd. *American Documents: The Bill of Rights*. Des Moines, IA: National Geographic Children's Books, 2006.

BIBLIOGRAPHY

American Civil Liberties Union. "Due Process." Retrieved March 2010 (http://www.aclu.org/immigrants-rights/due-process).

Blair Smith, Elliot. "PG&E Critic Erin Brockovich Doubtful About Legal Settlement." *USA Today*, February 6, 2006. Retrieved March 2010 (http://www.usatoday.com/money/industries/energy/2006-02-06-pge-settlement-brockovich_x.htm).

Buck, Anna. "A Primer on the 7th Amendment." ProtectConsumer Justice.org, September 17, 2009. Retrieved March 2010 (http://www.protectconsumerjustice.org/a-primmer-on-the-7th-amendment.html).

CriminalDefenseLawyer.com. "Laws on Tampering with Evidence." Retrieved March 2010 (http://www.criminaldefenselawyer.com/crime-penalties/federal/Tampering-with-evidence.htm).

El-Rahman, Minara. "Toyota Lawsuit Over Sudden Acceleration Picks Up Speed." FindLaw.com, November 11, 2009. Retrieved March 2010 (http://blogs.findlaw.com/injured/2009/11/toyota-lawsuit-picks-up-speed.html).

FreeAdvice.com. "Suing Being Sued." Retrieved March 2010 (http://law.freeadvice.com/general_practice/suing_being_sued/suit_options.htm).

Kowalski, Kathiann M. *Order in the Court: A Look at the Judicial Branch*. Minneapolis, MN: Lerner Publications Company, 2004.

LawFirms.com. "Differences Between Criminal and Civil Litigation Cases." Retrieved March 2010 (http://www.lawfirms.com/resources/lawsuits-and-disputes/litigation/differences-between-criminal-and-civil-litigation.htm).

Oldham, James. *Trial by Jury: The Seventh Amendment and Anglo-American Special Juries*. New York, NY: New York University Press, 2006.

Roach, Marilyn. *The Salem Witch Trials: A Day-by-Day Chronicle of a Community Under Siege*. New York, NY: Cooper Square Press, 2002.

Sack, Kevin. "Whistle-Blowing Nurse Is Acquitted in Texas." *New York Times*, February 11, 2010. Retrieved March 2010 (http://www.nytimes.com/2010/02/12/us/12nurses.html).

Saltzman, Jonathan. "Woman Loses Second-Hand Smoke Case." *Boston Globe*, February 17, 2010. Retrieved March 2010 (http://www.boston.com/news/local/massachusetts/articles/2010/02/17/woman_loses_second_hand_smoke_case).

Silberdick Feinberg, Barbara. *Constitutional Amendments*. New York, NY: Henry Holt Press, 1996.

SixWise.com. "How Many Lawsuits Are There in the U.S. & What Are They For?" October 5, 2006. Retrieved March 2010 (http://www.sixwise.com/newsletters/06/10/05/how-many-lawsuits-are-there-in-the-us--amp-what-are-they-for-an-amazing-overview.htm).

Stolberg, Sheryl Gay, and Robert Pear. "Obama Considers Limiting Suits Against Doctors." SFGate.com, June 15, 2009. Retrieved March 2010 (http://articles.sfgate.com/2009-06-15/news/17208119_1_care-overhaul-ama-officials-health-care).

Troisi-Paton, Kimberly. *The Right to Due Process*. Farmington Hills, MI: Greenhaven Press, 2005.

VerdictSearch.com. "Carpenter Alleged Spine, Ankle Injuries from 15-Foot Fall." Retrieved March 2010 (http://www.verdictsearch.com/index.jsp?do=sample).

WiseGeek.com. "What Is the Seventh Amendment to the Constitution?" Retrieved March 2010 (http://www.wisegeek.com/what-is-the-seventh-amendment-to-the-us-constitution.htm).

INDEX

About the Author

Kathy Furgang has written numerous books relating to American history, government, and the law. She lives in upstate New York with her husband and two sons.

Photo Credits

Cover Ron Chapple/Taxi/Getty Images; cover (inset) © www.istockphoto.com/Rich Legg; p. 1 (top) © www.istockphoto.com/Tom Nulens; p. 1 (bottom) © www.istockphoto.com/Lee Pettet; p. 3 © www.istockphoto.com/Nic Taylor; pp. 4–5 Fuse/Getty Images; pp. 7, 20, 30, 40 © www.istockphoto.com/arturbo; p. 8 Joe Raedle/Getty Images; pp. 10–11 © Peabody Essex Museum, Salem, MA/Bridgeman Art Library; pp. 14–15 © Massachusetts Historical Society, Boston, MA/Bridgeman Art Library; pp. 16–17 Smithsonian American Art Museum, Washington, DC/Art Resource, NY; p. 21 Jim McIsaac/Getty Images; pp. 23, 26–27 Chip Somodevilla/Getty Images; p. 32 Getty Images; p. 35 Photodisc/Thinkstock; pp. 36–37 Comstock/Getty Images; pp. 42–43 David McNew/Getty Images; pp. 44–45 © AP Images; pp. 48–49 William Thomas Cain/Bloomberg/Getty Images.

Photo Researcher: Amy Feinberg